SOUTH WALES
RAILWAYS
IN THE 1980s

Kevin Redwood

AMBERLEY

First published 2020

Amberley Publishing
The Hill, Stroud
Gloucestershire, GL5 4EP

www.amberley-books.com

Copyright © Kevin Redwood, 2020

The right of Kevin Redwood to be identified
as the Author of this work has been asserted in
accordance with the Copyrights, Designs and
Patents Act 1988.

ISBN 978 1 4456 9581 5 (print)
ISBN 978 1 4456 9582 2 (ebook)

British Library Cataloguing in Publication Data.
A catalogue record for this book is available from
the British Library.

Origination by Amberley Publishing.
Printed in the UK.

Introduction

I was born into a railway family in Exeter and so developed an early love of trains. When I started at grammar school, I joined the grammar school railway society. I made my first visit to South Wales on 7 November 1970, when the first trip I went on was to the open day at Cardiff Canton. I remember we also went to Dai Woodham's scrapyard at Barry. Around that time, I made another trip to Barry, this time with my father, who spent his whole working life on the railway. One thing that struck me at the time was just how busy the South Wales main line was compared to our local network in Exeter. We spent some time at Cardiff Central, where there seemed to be DMUs departing every few minutes, and Newport, where I was fascinated at just how frequently signals would turn green, to be quickly followed by the passing of a freight train of some sort. I had never previously seen English Electric Type 3 diesels, or Class 37s as they were later known.

I joined BR in 1977 straight from school. In 1978 my interest in freight traffic led me to a job in the Bristol Area Freight Centre as a TOPS clerk. There I quickly learned how much freight traffic originated in South Wales. I bought a copy of the Baker *Rail Atlas* and like the author, Stuart Baker, was bewildered by all the 'Llans' and 'Abers'. In 1980 I purchased my first basic SLR camera and started taking more photos, and because of my interest in freight trains I made many visits to South Wales. Most of my visits were made on weekdays and I usually travelled alone armed with my Baker *Rail Atlas* and a local OS map, both of which were invaluable. I have never been particularly interested in the glamorous high-profile side of the railway industry; instead I prefer the mundane everyday operations which were the railway's bread and butter. I tried to visit locations with plenty of freight activity; a dull day or a bit of rain did not put me off. All the photos in this book were taken by me between 1980 and 1986, across the South Wales Division of the Western Region.

The South Wales Division had its headquarters at Cardiff Queen Street and covered all the lines in South Wales. It also included the Central Wales route and the north and west route as far north as Craven Arms. The South Wales main line was the busiest route with an InterCity HST service from Paddington to Swansea, with some services extended further west. There was also a limited cross-country service. Loco-hauled trains ran on the Cardiff to Manchester route, and also the Cardiff to Portsmouth Harbour route, which gained in importance during the decade. DMU services were operated from Cardiff eastwards to Bristol, Gloucester and Cheltenham as well as on an extensive network in the Cardiff Valleys. Swansea was also the hub of services worked by DMUs to West Wales, and over the Central Wales route.

Freight traffic was particularly important to the division, which handled a much greater tonnage than on the rest of the Western Region. The principal commodities were coal, steel, and petroleum products. Coal was forwarded from over thirty collieries and washeries, as well as a number of stocking and blending sites and coke ovens. A lot of coal was moved from collieries to washeries and coke works, meaning that in places loaded coal trains could pass one another heading in opposite directions. Major coal customers were British Steel plants at Margam and Llanwern, the power station at Aberthaw, as well as for export via the docks at Swansea and Barry. There was also domestic coal to coal concentration depots across the BR network, though this was in sharp decline.

The British Steel plants at Margam and Llanwern dispatched products to numerous customers using a wide variety of wagon types. There were also many train movements between the steel plants and to the BSC tinplate works at Ebbw Vale, Trostre, and Velindre.

Petroleum products came principally from the three refineries in Milford Haven, at Robeston, Waterston, and Herbrandston. There was also petroleum traffic from other locations including Llandarcy, as well as chemical traffic to and from Baglan Bay.

Freight marshalling yards were located at Severn Tunnel Junction, A. D. (Alexandra Dock) Junction, Radyr, Margam, and Llandeilo Junction. The traditional vacuum-braked wagon-load network was being run down and finally ceased in 1984, scrap and domestic coal being the last regular traffic to be conveyed. The replacement Speedlink network connected yards and terminals across the network, and Severn Tunnel Junction was an important yard with direct services to all regions of BR.

The two main loco depots were at Cardiff Canton and Swansea Landore. Each had a large allocation including shunting locos as well as many Class 37s and 47s, and there were Class 56s allocated to Canton. Smaller depots at Ebbw Junction and Margam had an allocation of shunting locos for local yards. There was also a small depot at Severn Tunnel Junction to service locos arriving at the busy yards there. There were a number of other loco stabling points across the division where traincrew were also based, including Radyr, Llanelli, and Pantyffynnon. The DMU fleet was allocated to Cardiff Canton, and most of the suburban sets were based there, although some were stabled overnight at other locations including Rhymney and Treherbert. Many of the cross-country DMUs, and later the Class 101 sets, were out-based at Swansea for use in West Wales.

Compiling this book has brought back many happy memories of my trips to South Wales. On my visits I often had helpful advice both from railway staff and members of the public, and so I remember the time with fondness. My father Norman Redwood worked for the WR civil engineers and I sometimes accompanied him when he was visiting yards and depots. My friend and BR colleague, Roland Carp, accompanied me on a few of the trips where he did the driving. I must also thank my mother Ruth for taking me to 'see the trains' when I was little, and my partner Antoinette for her support and encouragement when compiling my books.

The extensive marshalling yards at Severn Tunnel Junction were served by Class 08 shunting locos, five or six locos being out-based, initially from Ebbw Junction depot. As well as shunting the yards, one pilot duty also shunted the Silcock & Colling car terminal located at the site of the former steam shed. On 16 June 1983 No. 08652 propels three loaded cartic sets through the station. The single VEA is possibly destined for the MOD sidings at Caerwent.

Most wagonload freight trains called at Severn Tunnel Junction and many trains were hump shunted. On 9 September 1980 No. 08932 has just finished propelling a train over the Down hump and stands outside the Down hump cabin. Pilot No. 08932 was one of the large number allocated to Ebbw Junction, while No. 31209 was an Old Oak Common-allocated loco.

A road bridge spanned the main lines and part of the yard at Severn Tunnel Junction. The Down hump yard is seen from the bridge on 9 September 1980. The concrete pad in the foreground was used for wagon repairs; a small crane stands on the adjacent siding. Many of the wagons are vacuum-braked examples, though a number of air-braked vehicles are also present, some in the newly introduced flame red livery.

The traditional vacuum-braked wagon-load network lasted until 1984; household coal was an important traffic right to the end, as seen in this view on 16 June 1983. A service for Acton departs Severn Tunnel Junction behind No. 47064. The first wagon is a recently converted turbot (TOPS code YCV), one of a large number converted for the civil engineers' department, and it is wearing the newly introduced 'dutch' livery.

Severn Tunnel Junction was an important yard on the Speedlink network, with services running on five of the thirteen Speedlink trunk routes. Route 10 was South Wales to Harwich. On 25 September 1986, the 6E82 18.20 Severn Tunnel Junction to Whitemoor departs Severn Tunnel Junction hauled by Thornaby-allocated No. 47303. House coal in air-braked hoppers (TOPS coded HEA) forms a significant part of the load.

With trains from all regions of BR arriving and departing Severn Tunnel Junction it was not surprising that a wide variety of locos could be seen there. Outside the depot, on 16 June 1983, are Crewe Diesel-allocated Nos 25257 and 25164. From Toton depot are No. 45127 and a pair of Class 20s, Nos 20141 and 20136.

On the Up side at Severn Tunnel Junction the Up hump yard was double-ended, and to the north of that lay the single-ended Up storage sidings, also known as the Bristol Yard. Outside the cabin, on 9 September 1980, are two of the yard pilots. On the left is Up hump yard pilot No. 08848, and on the right Bristol Yard pilot No. 08780, which is shunting a rake of dogfish ballast hoppers.

The most westerly yard at Severn Tunnel Junction was the Up reception sidings, also known as Undy Yard. Looking east on 25 September 1986, the Undy Yard contains a loaded MGR set from Oakdale to Scunthorpe, and a long rake of air-braked vans. The ground frame is built in the later Western Region timber design, sometimes referred to as plywood style. The Severn Tunnel Junction yards closed in 1987.

In 1976 BR had introduced a fleet of air-braked hoppers for domestic and industrial coal traffic, initially TOPS-coded HBA. Some of the fleet received modified suspension and were able to run at 60 mph, so could travel on Speedlink services; these were recoded HEA. On 16 June 1983, No. 37268 arrives at Undy Yard with three empty HEAs from the Gwent Coal Concentration Depot in Newport. Commencing in November 1986, all remaining domestic coal depots were served by the new Speedlink Coal Network.

On 25 September 1986 Eastleigh-allocated No. 33026 is seen passing Undy Yard with the 12.10 Portsmouth Harbour to Cardiff Central. The Southern Region-based Class 33s had taken over the Portsmouth Harbour services from Bath Road-allocated Class 31/4s in May 1980. The service on this route had comprised just seven trains each weekday from Portsmouth to Bristol, but by 1986 there were fourteen trains on weekdays, nine of which ran through to Cardiff.

Heading west from Severn Tunnel Junction the South Wales main line is four-tracked. On 16 June 1983 a pair of Crewe Diesel-allocated locos, Nos 25257 and 25164, head west past Undy Yard on the Down relief line with loaded dogfish ballast hoppers. Behind the locos is ballast plough No. DS62523, built by the SECR as long ago as 1914. Vacuum-braked only, No. 25164 would be withdrawn from traffic within two months.

On 16 June 1983, accelerating westwards past Undy on the Down relief line, is one of Cardiff Canton depot's large allocation of Class 37s, No. 37268. The fully fitted train of empty coal wagons comprises types MCV/MXV, HTV, and MDV, which were otherwise known as 16-ton minerals, 21-ton hoppers and 21-ton minerals.

In the early 1980s the stations at Lydney, Chepstow and Caldicot were served by a sporadic service of eight or nine trains each way a day between Cardiff and Gloucester or Cheltenham. On the Down main line at Undy, on 16 June 1983, is the 12.07 from Cheltenham Spa to Cardiff Central. Class 116 Derby suburban set C300 is formed of vehicle Nos 53080, 59030 and 53122.

By 1983 many parts of the BR network had become a fully fitted railway, but in South Wales some partly fitted or unfitted trains would continue to run until 1987. On 16 June 1983 Landore-allocated No. 37304 is working 9A75 from Severn Tunnel Junction to A. D. Junction with a very mixed load formed of both vacuum-braked and air-braked vehicles. Behind the loco is coal in MDVs, then a couple of engineer's wagons, followed by steel empties of type BAA or BBA, and more coal in HTVs with a brake van at the rear.

The 12.40 Cardiff Central to Gloucester local service is formed by a Class 101 Met-Cam DMU, seen on the Up main line at Undy on 16 June 1983. Set C822 (formed of vehicle Nos 51495, 59096, and 51510) was one of fifteen Met-Cam sets based at Cardiff Canton at the time.

At the start of the decade there were no named Class 37s, but by 1983 No. 37180 *County of Dyfed/Sir Dyfed* was one of seven members of the class to carry names, having been named in May 1981. On 16 June 1983 it is seen heading west at Undy with an empty MGR set for Oakdale colliery which will then be loaded with coking coal for BSC Scunthorpe.

When Llanwern Works opened in 1962 it was originally known as Spencer Works. The huge site to the east of Newport stretched for 3 miles along the south side of the main line. On 10 February 1982, Bescot-allocated No. 31149 heads west past the BSC Llanwern Works with a train of BDAs loaded with steel billets.

Llanwern Works had no access by sea, so imported iron ore arrived by rail. From the mid-1970s it came from Port Talbot Docks. The trains, each formed of twenty-seven bogie tipplers, had been hauled by triple-headed Class 37s, until 1979 when pairs of Class 56s took over the work. On 10 February 1982, an empty ore set hauled by Nos 56043 and 56035 *Taff Merthyr* approaches the main line at Llanwern Works West Connection.

In South Wales one of the formations of a typical freight train of the early 1980s would be a Class 37 hauling a rake of 21-ton mineral wagons, either fitted (MDV) or unfitted (MDO). The BSC works at Llanwern was a major consumer of coking coal, much of it supplied from collieries in the Western Valleys of Gwent. At Llanwern Works West Connection, No. 37204 is seen held on the Up relief line on 10 February 1982 waiting access onto the works lines with a long train of loaded MDVs.

East Usk yard in Newport acted as a focal point for coal empties in the area, as well as receiving wagons from nearby Llanwern Works. Coal empties came from depots across the West of England and southern counties. The empties were then sent to collieries as required. On 10 February 1982, No. 37229 departs East Usk with a local trip from A. D. Junction to Severn Tunnel Junction.

The signal box at East Usk Junction, which controlled access to the Uskmouth branch with semaphore signals, was a survivor in an area where the main lines were controlled by Newport Panel signal box with colour light signals. A train of coal (in MDVs) for Llanwern restarts from the Up relief line behind No. 37270 on 10 February 1982.

The South Wales division also included the north and west route, via Hereford, to a regional boundary with the LMR at Craven Arms. As well as a passenger service between Cardiff Central and Manchester Piccadilly there was heavy freight traffic over the north and west route. On 12 February 1982, a vacuum-braked wagon-load freight service for Severn Tunnel Junction arrives at Hereford behind No. 47129.

An engineering train stands on the Down relief at Hereford behind No. 37308, waiting a pathway to head south on 12 February 1982. In the platform stands Class 117 Pressed Steel DMU set L424 (formed of vehicle Nos 51362, 59514, and 51404), which had just arrived on the 09.05 service from Oxford.

Class 37s were seen across South Wales throughout the 1980s. At the start of the decade the allocation of Class 37s was over ninety locos, split between Cardiff Canton and Swansea Landore depots. One of the Cardiff Canton allocation, No. 37224, is seen at Maindee West Junction in Newport on 7 May 1985.

Local services on the South Wales main line were worked by DMU sets allocated to both Cardiff and Bristol. Bristol-based Class 118 BRCW suburban set B474 is working the 06.38 service from Swindon to Cardiff Central via Gloucester, and is seen crossing the River Usk on the approach to Newport on 7 May 1985.

One service that continued to see Class 50s working passenger services in South Wales in the 1980s was the 08.57 Cardiff Central to Paddington. The loco and stock for this train were booked to work in on the 06.42 Weston-super-Mare to Cardiff Central each weekday. On 7 May 1985, the 08.57 from Cardiff was worked by 50043 *Eagle* and is seen crossing the River Usk shortly after departure from Newport.

On a grey morning on 23 February 1983 passenger trains meet on the River Usk viaduct at Newport. On the Up main is 1A77, the 06.47 Carmarthen to Paddington HST service, while heading west is a Class 117 Pressed Steel DMU working 2C16, the 07.44 service from Gloucester to Cardiff Central.

Inter-works steel between various BSC plants in South Wales was an important traffic for BR. On 7 May 1985 No. 37236 crosses the River Usk at Newport with steel slabs from Port Talbot to Llanwern. The wagons are a mix of BBA and BAA steel carriers.

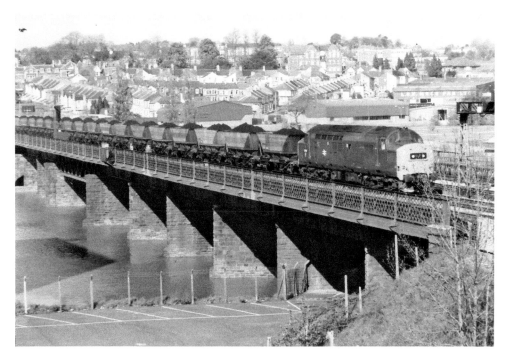

An MGR train of coking coal from Oakdale colliery to the British Steel plant at Scunthorpe crosses the River Usk behind No. 37187 on 7 May 1985. The Class 37 would only work the train to Severn Tunnel Junction, where the wagons would then be stabled to be worked forward to Scunthorpe overnight.

The twelve members of Class 33/2 had been built with narrow bodies to operate through the narrower tunnels on the Tonbridge to Hastings route in Kent. It was rare to see them on the Western Region in the early 1980s, so No. 33206 approaching Newport with the 19.30 Bristol Temple Meads to Cardiff Central on 24 May 1983 was an unusual event.

On 12 July 1985, No. 31117 heads westwards through Newport on the Down relief line with a train of four-wheel tanks. This loco was one of the first members of the class to be allocated to the Western Region when it was transferred to Old Oak Common in 1968.

The three Milford Haven oil refineries, at Robeston, Herbrandston and Waterston, generated a large amount of traffic for BR. Discharged tanks for the Gulf refinery at Waterston head through Newport behind No. 47374 on 12 July 1985.

In the early 1980s it was common for civil engineers' on-track equipment to be moved during the week on normal wagon-load services. A twin jib crane and associated mess coach, No. DW150401, forms part of 8C30, the 10.30 Margam to Severn Tunnel Junction, which is seen passing through Newport behind No. 47146 on 21 July 1982.

Cardiff Canton-allocated No. 37243 was unusual in having the loco number displayed on the nose ends for several years. On 12 July 1985 it was also sporting non-standard white window surrounds as it accelerated eastwards through Newport with a loaded coal train. The following year the loco went to Crewe Works for refurbishment and was re-numbered No. 37697.

Class 25s had been allocated to both Cardiff Canton and Ebbw Junction depots during the 1970s, although by the start of the 1980s there were none allocated; they were, however, still regular visitors to South Wales. They were often seen on parcels services including 4V20, the 15.20 Manchester Piccadilly to Bristol Temple Meads, which called at Newport to detach traffic and reverse. On 24 May 1983, No. 25266 of Cricklewood depot is seen on platform 1 at Newport while running around 4V20.

Following the closure of Ebbw Junction depot in 1982, locos were stabled at Godfrey Road, adjacent to Newport station. There were a number of Class 08 duties in the Newport area and two locos, Nos 08835 and 08634, are seen heading on to the stabling point on the evening of 4 September 1984.

HSTs had replaced loco-hauled stock on Paddington to South Wales services in 1977. By the 1980s, the pattern of service on weekdays was for departures on the hour from Paddington to Swansea during the day. The 12.00 Paddington to Swansea is seen at Newport on 25 September 1986 with power car No. 43171 in the lead.

One of Canton's large allocation of Class 47s, No. 47226, is seen on the Down relief line at Newport. It is heading west on 4 September 1984 with a train of discharged 100-ton bogie tank wagons (TOPS code TEA).

The South Wales main line was very busy, and at Newport seldom did more than a few minutes pass before another freight train or engine ran through the station. Passing beneath the gantry, on a grey 23 February 1983, is No. 37296 heading light diesel to Llanwern BSC on the Up relief line.

Immediately west of Newport station the four-track main line passes through a pair of tunnels. Here, on 7 May 1985, No. 37243 crosses to the Up main, and is about to enter Newport New Tunnel with loaded BBA steel carriers of coil from Llanwern to Ebbw Vale tinplate works.

Bursting into the sunshine at Gaer Junction on 7 May 1985 is Eastleigh-allocated No. 33026, with the 07.19 Manchester Piccadilly to Cardiff Central service. The Southern Region Class 33s had taken over services on the Cardiff to Manchester route from Crewe Diesel-allocated Class 25s in 1981.

Once the Class 33s had taken over the Portsmouth to Cardiff services in 1980, it was rare to see another class of loco working the Portsmouth to Bristol leg, but other classes did sometimes appear between Bristol and Cardiff. On 7 May 1985, Toton-allocated No. 45142 exits Newport New Tunnel at Gaer Junction with the 08.10 Portsmouth Harbour to Cardiff Central.

Exiting Newport Old Tunnel on the Down relief line at Gaer Junction on 7 May 1985 is No. 37176. The train is a Llanwern to Margam service and the first two wagons are loaded with steel coil for the BSC tinplate works at Trostre.

The heaviest trains in South Wales at the time were the iron ore trains from Port Talbot docks to Llanwern steelworks. The trains had been worked by pairs of Canton-allocated Class 56s since 1979, this being the first allocation of the class to the Western Region. On 7 May 1985, Nos 56047 and 56040 *Oystermouth* pass Gaer Junction with a loaded ore set.

From May 1982, Class 33s started working passenger services into West Wales to replace steam-heated Class 37 diagrams. Eastleigh-allocated Class 33 No. 33027 *Earl Mountbatten of Burma* passes Gaer Junction with the 07.40 Milford Haven to Bristol Temple Meads service on 7 May 1985.

Unfitted freight trains continued to run in South Wales after other parts of the BR network had become fully fitted. Export coil was one of the last traffic flows to utilise unfitted wagons on the short journey from Llanwern to Newport Docks. On 1 December 1981, No. 37176 heads west past Gaer Junction towards A. D. Junction, and then Newport Docks. This train is formed of coil J wagons, which were rebuilds of iron ore tipplers.

A number of collieries in the Western Valleys supplied coking coal to Llanwern including Marine, Oakdale and Rose Heyworth. An unidentified Class 37 hauls 6A82, the 09.45 Marine to Llanwern, through Gaer Junction on 23 February 1983; the lengthy train is composed of MDVs.

Domestic coal was one of the last traffics to pass on the vacuum-braked wagon-load network, which finally closed in 1984. From then, the remaining domestic coal depots now received coal in air-braked HEAs, via the Speedlink newtwork. On 7 May 1985, a Speedlink service from Coedbach to Severn Tunnel Junction passes Gaer Junction behind No. 37171. Behind the loco is a coal container loaded on a FPA, while the rest of the train is made up of HEAs.

At the start of the decade there were four quarries in South Wales supplying track ballast to BR, at Tintern and Tidenham, near Chepstow, Hirwaun, north of Aberdare, and Machen, to the west of Newport. On 7 May 1985, No. 37208 approaches Gaer Junction with a loaded ballast train from Machen; the train comprises twelve dogfish hoppers and a single sealion.

On 25 September 1986, an unidentified Class 37 starts the climb away from Gaer Junction towards Park Junction with a train of thirty empty MDVs for one of the Western Valley collieries. The working timetable for the period showed five trains to Marine Colliery and two to Oakdale on weekdays.

A train of coking coal for Llanwern, heading towards Gaer Junction, rounds the curve from Park Junction behind No. 37240 on 12 July 1985. Although the front portion of the train was formed of MDVs there was a rake of HTVs in the middle with more MDVs at the rear.

Track ballast from Machen quarry was of high quality and, after 1990, it was the only rail-served quarry in South Wales to supply track ballast. On 25 September 1986, No. 37181 rounds the curve from Park Junction at the head of a train of loaded dogfish hoppers from Machen.

An empty MGR train for Oakdale comprising twenty-one HAAs approaches Park Junction behind No. 37150 on 12 July 1985. The train is on the route from Ebbw Junction. In the past the track layout here was much more complex, with direct lines to Newport Docks; the track bed is on the left of the view.

On 12 July 1985 empty HAAs for Oakdale pass Park Junction signal box behind No. 37150. The box opened in 1885 and was later extended to house a 100-lever frame; at one time there were six lines running westwards from Park Junction to Bassaleg.

The BSC tinplate works at Ebbw Vale also provided inwards traffic for BR in the form of coil from Llanwern and elsewhere, as well as outwards tinplate traffic to various Metal Box locations. The 1986 freight WTT showed five booked trains arriving and departing on weekdays, all the services being 'Y' pathways from and to either Severn Tunnel Junction or Llanwern, as required. On 12 July 1985, No. 37185 heads through Park Junction with a service from Severn Tunnel Junction to Ebbw Vale. The six air-braked vans are a mix of types VAA, VBA and VCA.

On 25 September 1986, No. 37220 passes Park Junction with 7A67, the 11.40 from Oakdale to Llanwern, a lengthy train of coking coal loaded in HTVs.

Pit closures meant that the freight network had been contracting steadily, and the marshalling of the remaining traffic concentrated on fewer yards. Until the mid-1970s, Aberbeeg Yard supplied empty wagons to local collieries, and a number of Class 37s were out-based there. However, the yard was already closed by 1980. The Roath Dock Rumbler railtour passes Aberbeeg on 4 April 1981.

Rose Heyworth, near Abertillery, was one of the collieries that supplied Llanwern with coking coal. On 4 April 1981, the Roath Dock Rumbler railtour made a visit to Rose Heyworth. Bristol-based Class 118 BRCW DMUs B471 (formed of vehicle Nos 51314, 59481, and 51329) and B462 (formed of vehicle Nos 51304, 59477, and 51319) worked the railtour.

The Roath Dock Rumbler railtour also visited Waunllwyd sidings, which were the exchange sidings for the BSC tinplate works at Ebbw Vale. Class 118 BRCW DMUs B471 and B462 are seen at Waunllwyd on 4 April 1981.

At busy times trains could be held awaiting acceptance into various yards. On 19 May 1982, No. 37232 stands on the Down relief line west of Gaer Junction, waiting to enter A. D. (Alexandra Dock) Junction yard. Behind the loco is an air-braked SPA. However, the majority of the train is spoil or spent ballast, and is loaded in a variety of wagons, for the nearby Maesglas Tip.

On 12 July 1985, No. 37142 runs into A. D. Junction yard with a train of loaded HTVs of coal from Severn Tunnel Junction. The coal is for the Gwent Coal Distribution depot. No. 37142 will reverse here at A. D. Junction before continuing to the depot at Newport Dock Street.

With Waterloo Loop signal box in the background, No. 37426 *Y Lein Fach/Vale of Rheidol* cautiously rounds the curve with MDVs of coal for Newport Docks from Maesteg on 25 September 1986. No. 37426 is wearing large logo livery, having been converted and renumbered from No. 37299 in February 1986.

To serve Newport Docks and the other industries in the area, a very complex network of yards and sidings developed. Eastern Valley sidings were used for civil engineers' traffic, including spoil for the adjacent Maesglas tip. On 15 July 1980, the yard pilot is Ebbw Junction-allocated No. 08586.

A view looking east from the west end of A. D. Junction Yard on 12 July 1985. Declining traffic levels meant that the yard here was not busy at that time. However, two years later, when the yards at Severn Tunnel Junction were closed in 1987, the A. D. Junction yard took on an increased workload again.

A view from 19 May 1982 looking east at Ebbw Junction, with Ebbw Junction depot out of shot to the left, and A. D. Junction yard to the right. Five Class 37 locos are visible. An unidentified pair are stabled in Ebbw Junction sidings and No. 37306 has just come off the chord from Park Junction. No. 37290 was at the head of the train disappearing towards Newport, while No. 37268 is recessed in A. D. Junction yard, with MDVs of coking coal from Abertillery to BSC Grange sidings.

Ebbw Junction depot had an allocation of twenty-one Class 08 shunting locos in 1980, including No. 08481, seen inside the depot on 15 July 1980. Inside the shed is Canton-allocated No. 56045, while outside stands No. 47901 which, at the time, was a test-bed loco for the subsequent Class 58 fleet.

Standing in the sun, outside the west end of Ebbw Junction depot, on 25 January 1982 is Ebbw Junction-allocated No. 08822, alongside bufferless No. 37264 and No. 37301. The depot was to close later that same year and locos were then stabled at Godfrey Road, adjacent to Newport station.

Class 31/4s had been the regular performers on the Portsmouth Harbour route before the introduction of Class 33s on the workings in 1980. The Class 31s still deputised on occasions. Bath Road-allocated No. 31419 approaches Ebbw Junction with the 09.05 Cardiff Central to Bristol Temple Meads service on 19 May 1982.

There were two Freightliner terminals in South Wales, one at Swansea Danygraig, and one at Pengam, to the east of Cardiff. At Pengam, on 17 September 1981, No. 45015 shunts to form Up trains for that day's departures. At that date, departing services were 4E88 to Newcastle, 4E70 to Stratford, and 4S81 to Coatbridge.

The Tremorfa Steel Works and Castle Rod Mill at Cardiff were owned by Allied Steel & Wire and generated a lot of traffic for BR. On 17 September 1981, Canton-allocated No. 08352 is seen at Pengam sidings with nine BDAs loaded with steel billets which are being moved between the two plants.

Gateshead-allocated No. 47416 passes Newtown Yard in Cardiff with 3A03, the 12.50 Swansea to Paddington Premium Parcels, on 17 September 1981. On the left, Newtown Yard contains mostly condemned unfitted wagons that were on their way to Woodham's scrapyard at Barry. Newtown Yard itself closed in early 1982. On the right is Newtown NCL depot, which, by 1981, was no longer rail-connected.

Descending the bank from Cardiff Queen Street into Cardiff Central on 7 May 1985 are Nos 37235 and 37223 with a loaded MGR train for Aberthaw power station. Aberthaw received coal from a number of locations, and this train could have come from either Penallta colliery, Cwmbargoed opencast site, or the Ocean complex of collieries.

Approaching journey's end at Cardiff Central, behind No. 33030 is 1V26, the 12.10 departure from Portsmouth Harbour, on 8 February 1982. In 1980 Class 33s had taken over the loco diagrams on this route and would continue to work the Portsmouth Harbour services until replaced by Class 155 Super Sprinters, in May 1988.

Freight traffic through Cardiff Central was very heavy, with loaded coal trains heading both east and west. On 17 September 1981, No. 37230 heads west through platform 4 with coal for Nantgarw coking ovens. This train would be routed via the City Line to Radyr.

Although not as frequent as the HST service to London, there was a limited cross-country InterCity service from South Wales. On 21 July 1982, Bescot-allocated No. 47476 stands at Cardiff Central at the head of 1M11, the 07.50 Swansea to Manchester Piccadilly service.

Cardiff Canton had a large allocation of Class 116 Derby-built suburban DMUs for services in the Cardiff Valleys; there were twenty sets on the books at the start of the decade. On 14 April 1983, a pair of Class 116 DMUs have arrived empty from Canton to take up afternoon commuter services. The farthest set will depart on the 16.00 service to Aber, while set C312 (formed of vehicle Nos 50843, 59355, and 50896) will depart at 16.13 for Treherbert.

Bath Road-allocated Class 31s had a well-deserved reputation for being in poor external condition, and No. 31424 was no exception when seen at Cardiff Central on 9 September 1980. The train was the 07.46 Portsmouth Harbour to Cardiff Central. Since May that year Class 33s had been diagrammed to the route, but locos of other classes were often seen on the Bristol to Cardiff leg.

To convey engine parts and stores between main works and diesel depots there was an Enparts network that had used former coaching stock. However, with the advent of the Speedlink Network a pool of VCAs was allocated to the work. At Cardiff Central on 15 June 1983, the shunter detaches two VCAs for Canton depot from the rear of a westbound Speedlink working for Barry to be taken to the depot by No. 31117.

Stock off the Portsmouth to Cardiff services went to Canton depot for servicing before the next return working. On 14 April 1983, empty stock for the 16.15 to Portsmouth Harbour snakes across the pointwork into Cardiff Central behind No. 33031.

23 miles north of Cardiff Central is Rhymney, which had been a terminus since closure of the route northwards to Rhymney Bridge in 1954. The train pattern varied over the years but generally consisted of thirteen or fourteen weekday departures to Cardiff Central, Penarth, or Barry. On 22 May 1980, refurbished Class 117/116/117 set C454 (formed of vehicle Nos 51352, 59359, and 51394) waits at Rhymney before working 2C51, the 09.20 Rhymney to Penarth.

A pair of Class 37s, Nos 37255 and 37300, stand in the long-closed remains of Trelewis Halt while the rear of the MGR train is loaded by mechanical shovel at Deep Navigation colliery on 24 May 1983. Once loading is complete, the train of twenty-eight HAAs will depart for Aberthaw power station.

The Ocean complex of collieries included Deep Navigation, Taff Merthyr, and Trelewis Drift. As well as coal there was also colliery shale to be moved to the tip at Nelson Bog. Each weekday there was a local trip duty to shuttle between the collieries and Nelson Bog. On 24 May 1983, No. 37251 is on shale duty and brings empties through the site of Trelewis Halt.

With Deep Navigation colliery in the background, No. 37251 shunts a train of colliery shale. The wagons are 34-ton former iron ore hoppers with a TOPS code of HKV. These hoppers were originally used for imported iron ore from Newport Docks to Llanwern.

On the Valley lines a number of peak-hour trains were booked to terminate at various stations in the suburbs of Cardiff, such as Llandaff. Cardiff-based Class 116 set C316 (formed of vehicle Nos 50856, 59364 and 50909) had terminated at Llandaff on a service from Cardiff Central. It is seen crossing over to the Down platform, prior to working the 08.55 service back to Cardiff on 26 June 1981.

A wagon type not commonly seen in South Wales in the past was the 24-ton hopper (with a TOPS code of HUO). In the early 1980s a large number of the type were transferred to South Wales as replacements for life-expired coke hoppers; they were used for export traffic through Barry Docks. Departing Radyr on 3 November 1981 is No. 37235 with empty HUOs for Nantgarw coking plant.

The ARC quarry at Penderyn was reached via a junction at Hirwaun. At the start of the 1980s it was one of the suppliers of track ballast to the WR. Ballast from Penderyn was mostly used on branch lines and in West Wales. On 23 November 1982, No. 37222 heads north through Radyr with dogfish hoppers and a shark plough van for Hirwaun. During the 1980s ballast loading ceased, and the line from Hirwaun to Penderyn was subsequently lifted.

Radyr Yard was the major marshalling yard serving the Cardiff Valleys. As well as Canton-allocated Class 08 yard pilots, there were also a number of Class 37s out-based here for local freight trip work. Two Canton-allocated Class 37s are seen at Radyr on 28 November 1980. Waiting acceptance into the yard is No. 37248 with a coal train, while No. 37286 departs the yard light diesel.

On 11 August 1982, No. 37273 cautiously approaches Radyr with a local trip of coal from Tymawr colliery loaded in a mix of MDVs, an MDO, MCVs and a brake van. The goods-only Down relief line from Walnut Tree Junction to Radyr Junction was signalled by Permissive Block, and at busy times trains could be queued up here awaiting access into Radyr Yard.

The Taff Vale route from Cardiff north to Pontypridd had been quadrupled to handle the huge tonnage of coal that once went for export from numerous collieries. On 11 August 1982, Class 116 set C307 heads north on the Up main, having just passed beneath the M4 bridge at Morganstown with the 08.18 service from Barry to Taffs Well.

By the early 1980s, although the Down relief line was still in regular use between Radyr and Taffs Well, the Up relief line has a coating of rust, as seen from Morganstown foot crossing. The 08.20 service from Treherbert to Barry Island approaches the crossing on 11 August 1982. Class 116 set C320 is formed of vehicle Nos 50869, 59035 and 50922.

Shipment coke from the Nantgarw coking plant to Barry Docks in HUOs is the load for No. 37285, seen approaching Morganstown on 11 August 1982. Castell Coch looks down on the scene from across the River Taff. The unfitted 24.5-ton HUOs had replaced coke hoppers on coke traffic in South Wales.

The Rhondda valleys had been one of the most important coal mining regions but by the start of the 1980s few collieries remained, and only Maerdy and Tymawr remained rail-connected. On 11 August 1982, No. 37273 approaches Taffs Well on the Up main line with empties from Radyr for Tymawr.

On 11 August 1982, the 08.53 service from Barry Island to Treherbert approaches Taffs Well, formed by Class 116 set C320. The surviving pier of Walnut Tree viaduct is still showing the decoration applied in 1977 to mark the silver jubilee of Queen Elizabeth II.

At Taffs Well, Walnut Tree Junction signal box controlled a connection off the Taff Vale main line onto the branch up the Big Hill towards Aber. It also controlled a later connection into Nantgarw colliery and coke works, just north of the station. On 26 June 1981, No. 37270 heads south with empties from Nantgarw. Following colliery closures in the Rhymney Valley reduced freight traffic meant that the Aber branch closed in 1982.

On 3 November 1981, a train of empty MDVs has just been brought out of Nantgarw by No. 37235 and has come to a stand in the platform at Taffs Well. The signalman has just collected the train staff. The loco was one of the Canton Class 37 allocation that was still vacuum-braked only at the time.

The morning peak train service sees two Class 116 Derby-built suburban sets at Taffs Well on 11 August 1982. Set C302 (formed of vehicle Nos 50086, 59036, and 50128) has just arrived and terminated with the 08.18 Saturdays excepted service from Barry. Meanwhile, set C334 (formed of vehicle Nos 51139, 59033, and 51152) is working the 08.20 Treherbert to Barry Island service.

Canton-allocated No. 37271 creeps cautiously southwards through Taffs Well, heading for Radyr Yard with a train of loaded MCVs on 26 June 1981. Smoke is issuing from the eighth wagon, MCV No. B587638, which has a hot axle box and will be detached in the yard at Radyr.

In 1952 a new connection was made from the Taff Vale main line, just north of Taffs Well, to serve Nantgarw colliery, which had previously been served by the Cardiff Railway route from Heath Junction. As well as being used by trains to and from the colliery and coke works, the connection was used to enable DMUs terminating at Taffs Well to reverse. On 11 August 1982, set C302 re-joins the main line, running empty to form the 09.17 Taffs Well to Cardiff Central service.

When there were still many unfitted wagons in use it had been common practice for engines engaged on local trip work in the Valleys to work with a brake van for the duration of the shift. On 24 May 1983, No. 37279 propels a brake van southward towards Radyr Yard, past the Nantgarw colliery connection.

The wide track bed is evidence that the Taff Vale main line had been four-tracked between Radyr and Pontypridd. Class 116 set C338 is seen just after departure from Taffs Well, working the 17.38 service from Penarth to Abercynon on 24 May 1983.

There had been four tracks between Radyr and Pontypridd, but declining freight traffic meant that the relief lines were taken out of use between Taffs Well and Pontypridd in 1980, and subsequently lifted. The 16.52 Merthyr Tydfil to Penarth service is seen just north of Taffs Well on 24 May 1983. Class 116 set C313 is formed of vehicle Nos 50847, 59040, and 50900.

Treforest Estate station was opened in 1942 to serve the workers of Treforest Industrial Estate. This area had grown as new factories were set up to help with the war effort. The 10.52 Cardiff Central to Merthyr Tydfil calls on 3 November 1981; the service is worked by Class 116 set C301, which is formed of vehicle Nos 50084, 59373, and 50126.

Pontypridd station consisted of a single large island platform with goods lines to the west, having been rebuilt in that configuration in the early twentieth century. A Class 116 set in refurbished livery, and on a service from Merthyr Tydfil, calls on 22 May 1980. Set C318 is formed of vehicle Nos 50917, 59369, and 50864.

The Taff Vale Railway main line was from Cardiff to Merthyr; a branch to the Rhondda Valleys diverges at Pontypridd. On 3 November 1981 a Rhondda Valley service from Cardiff to Treherbert departs from Pontypridd. Set C454 is a hybrid set formed of Class 117/116/117 vehicle Nos 51352, 59359, and 51394.

Although the yards at Stormstown had been heavily rationalised by the start of the 1980s the remaining loops and sidings were still in use, principally by coal traffic. Lady Windsor colliery was accessed by a freight-only branch from here. On 24 May 1983, the 08.52 Barry Island to Merthyr Tydfil service passes the yards. Class 117 set C317 is formed of vehicle Nos 50858, 59446, and 50911.

Standing in the Up yard at Stormstown on 24 May 1983 is No. 37231 with coal from Lady Windsor colliery loaded in MDVs and HTVs. The train is awaiting a path to proceed north to the phurnacite plant at Abercwmboi, which received coal for processing from a variety of sources.

Coal from Merthyr Vale colliery to Abercwmboi ran via Stormstown, where trains were required to reverse. On 24 May 1983, No. 37239 has already run round the train of MDVs and MCVs and is now departing northwards for Abercwmboi.

The station at Abercynon had been originally named Aberdare Junction when it first opened. The branch to Aberdare can be seen curving away to the left. The main line north to Merthyr Tydfil climbs steeply from the end of the platform; to the right of the island platform is a lengthy sand drag. Class 116 set C317 calls at the platform with the 10.49 Merthyr Tydfil to Penarth service on 24 May 1983.

On 14 April 1983, Landore-allocated No. 37180 heads through Abercynon with a lengthy rake of empty HTVs and HTOs for the National Smokeless Fuels phurnacite plant at Abercwmboi. In the background is the former Abercynon shed, which had closed to steam in 1964; it was now in industrial use.

Passenger services to Aberdare had ceased in 1964, a victim of the Beeching axe. To handle the remaining passenger service to Merthyr Tydfil a single platform face sufficed at Abercynon. On 24 May 1983, the signal man hands over the token for the single-line section to Black Lion. Class 116 DMU set C313 is working the 11.30 service from Penarth to Merthyr Tydfil.

On 14 April 1983 Class 116 DMU set C303 has just arrived at Abercynon with the 12.00 service from Merthyr Tydfil to Cardiff Central. The train service here improved three years later in 1988 as passenger services over the Aberdare branch resumed.

By 1980 Merthyr Vale was the only remaining rail-connected colliery in the valley; it was connected to the main line by a short steep branch up to Black Lion. On 14 April 1983, No. 37231 departs from Black Lion with MDVs and MCVs of coal for Abercwmboi. The train will run via Stormstown, where it will reverse.

Black Lion loop was the only crossing place on the single line between Abercynon and Merthyr Tydfil, the line having been singled in 1971. On 14 April 1983, Class 116 DMU set C313 is seen heading north at Black Lion loop on the 09.52 Cardiff Central to Merthyr Tydfil service.

At Merthyr Vale, the main line runs along the east side of the valley with Merthyr Vale colliery on the valley floor beside the River Taff. At the colliery were two former BR Class 08 shunting locos, Nos D3014 and D3183. On 14 April 1983, one of the pair is seen hauling coal in HTVs and MCVs from the colliery up to Black Lion.

One of the Cardiff-allocated Met-Cam DMUs passes Merthyr Vale colliery working the 10.00 Merthyr Tydfil to Cardiff Central on 14 April 1983. Set C811 is formed of vehicle Nos 51801, 59548, and 51519. The colliery closed in August 1989.

At Merthyr Vale the former Up line remained in use when the route was singled. Class 116 set C303 is seen again, this time calling at Merthyr Vale with the 12.00 Merthyr Tydfil to Cardiff Central service on 14 April 1983.

The station at Merthyr Tydfil had been rebuilt in 1974 with just two tracks either side of a single island platform. In the early 1980s though, the service to Cardiff on weekdays was roughly hourly with two-hour gaps in the early afternoon. On 22 May 1980, a refurbished Class 116 set waits to form the 12.00 service to Cardiff Central. Set C318 is formed of vehicle Nos 50864, 59369, and 50917.

In 1985 a number of the Class 116 sets allocated to Cardiff Canton received Valley Train markings (*Tren Y Cwm* in Welsh). Driving Motor Brake Second (DMBS) No. 53858, part of set C317, stands at Penarth on 7 May 1985. It had been renumbered from No. 50858 in May 1983, when all DMU stock in the 50XXX and 56XXX number ranges was renumbered as part of a scheme to add coaching stock to the TOPS system.

A northbound Class 116 DMU set, C313, calls at Cadoxton on 21 July 1982. In the distance is the connection into Barry Docks, where two Class 08s, including No. 08187, are visible together with a number of coal hoppers.

Approaching Barry is Class 116 set, in the recently introduced Valley Train markings. Set C332 (formed of vehicle Nos 51134, 59444, and 51147) is working the 14.13 service from Treherbert to Barry Island on 7 May 1985.

Class 116 set C307 was a hybrid set. The formation of vehicles changed over time but, on 21 July 1982, the set included two Driving Motor Brake Seconds (DMBS) when seen at Barry. The vehicle numbers are 50083, 59031, and 50820, and the service is the 10.53 from Barry Island to Merthyr Tydfil.

Pairs of Class 37s were out-based at Barry to work the MGR trains supplying Aberthaw power station. At times of high demand for coal, up to six or seven pairs of locos were required. On 7 May 1985 Nos 37223 and 37235 are seen in the sidings at Barry.

Aberthaw Cement was an important freight customer, forwarding cement from plants at Aberthaw and Rhoose, as well as receiving coal. On 7 May 1985, No. 47359 stands at Barry with a train of Aberthaw Cement PCAs. On the left is the rear of the former steam shed, which was then used for wagon repairs.

Barry Island had a hourly service with additional trains during the morning and afternoon peaks. On 21 July 1982, a Class 116 set departs Barry and rounds the curve towards Barry Island less than a mile away; the journey will take three minutes. Set C319 is formed of vehicle Nos 50868, 59371, and 50918.

At its peak the station at Barry Island once boasted four platforms, and trains would arrive and depart at five-minute intervals on bank holidays. However, the line from Barry had been singled in 1969 and a single platform sufficed for normal traffic. On 14 April 1981, Class 116 set C335 (formed of vehicle Nos 51140, 59032, and 51153) awaits departure time.

Coal trains to Aberthaw consisted of twenty-eight HAAs hauled by pairs of Class 37 locos. At Aberthaw reception sidings, the Class 37s were replaced by a slow-speed-fitted Class 47, which was required to haul the train round the power station loop for tipping. At the reception sidings on 12 November 1985 are Nos 37205 and 37240, which had just arrived with coal from Ogmore.

Cardiff Canton-allocated slow-speed-fitted Class 47 No. 47186 runs into the reception sidings at Aberthaw with an empty MGR set from the power station on 12 November 1985. Coal came from many sources over the years in South Wales, including collieries, washeries, and blending sites. In 1987 the Freight Train loads book listed Blaenant, Brynlliw, Cardiff Tidal, Cwmbargoed, Cwm Cynon, Deep Navigation, Jersey Marine, Lady Windsor, Merthyr Vale, Oakdale, Ocean/Deep Navigation, and Penallta.

Some of the coal from the opencast site at Llanharan went to Didcot power station loaded in HAAs. In the late afternoon on 12 November 1985, No. 37235 departs from Llantrisant with a loaded MGR train from Llanharan.

Stratford-allocated No. 37044 was an unusual performer on 3A03, the 12.22 Swansea to Paddington Premium Parcels service. It is seen calling at Bridgend on 6 November 1981.

Coal for Aberthaw, from loading points in the west at Blaenant, Brynlliw, and Jersey Marine, travelled via the Vale of Glamorgan route. Trains taking this route ran up through Bridgend station on the Down main line as far as Bridgend East Junction. On 7 July 1981, Nos 37231 and 37291 run through Bridgend with an MGR service for Aberthaw power station.

There were hourly HST departures from Swansea to Paddington during the day. Some early-morning departures started further west at Milford Haven, Haverfordwest or Carmarthen. The 11.45 Swansea to Paddington calls at Bridgend on 6 November 1981, formed by set No. 253020.

Margam depot was opened in 1964 to fuel and service locos from the new Margam Yard. The depot had an allocation of Class 08 shunting locos to cover duties in the marshalling yard; there were seven locos allocated in 1980. The view of the west end of the depot on 28 July 1980 sees a variety of visiting locos including Nos 46035, 37191, 37178, and 37300. Margam-allocated Nos 08366 and 08360 were also present.

Part of the massive BSC Port Talbot works dominates the skyline as No. 56036 heads west on the Down main line, approaching Port Talbot station, on 19 September 1986. The train of coil loaded on BAAs and BBAs is headed for the BSC tinplate works at Trostre.

Port Talbot station originally opened in 1850 and subsequently had several changes of name. It reverted to Port Talbot in 1947 before being renamed Port Talbot Parkway in 1984. On 7 July 1981, while simply named Port Talbot, HST set No. 253029 approaches, working the 14.42 service from Swansea to Paddington.

In May 1982 Southern Region Class 33s commenced working west of Cardiff, initially from Swansea to West Wales. By 1986 there were also services between Swansea and Portsmouth Harbour. On 19 September 1986, Class 33/2 No. 33206 runs into Port Talbot Parkway at the head of the 16.05 Swansea to Portsmouth Harbour service.

As well as the refineries at Milford Haven, petroleum traffic also originated from other sources. On 7 July 1981, Landore-allocated No. 37289 heads eastwards through Port Talbot with a train of 100-ton tank cars from the BP refinery at Llandarcy.

A loaded MGR train for Aberthaw power station approaches Port Talbot on 7 July 1981. Consecutively numbered Class 37s Nos 37304 and 37303 were two of the batch of locos fitted with modified draw-gear for working triple-headed on the Port Talbot iron ore services.

Neath station was formerly known as Neath General to distinguish it from the other three stations in the town, which had all closed in the 1960s. The 11.42 Swansea to Paddington service calls on 7 July 1981, formed by HST set No. 253018. HSTs would continue to operate services to Paddington until 2019.

The Neath train service was principally the hourly Paddington HSTs, augmented by a cross-country service in each direction and one additional peak-hour service to and from Cardiff. On 9 November 1983, the 14.30 Swansea to Paddington service calls at Neath, formed by HST set No. 253016. The blue and white sign by the hut on the left is a 'T' board, indicating the termination of a temporary speed restriction.

All of the South Wales DMU fleet was allocated to Cardiff Canton, though in practice a number of sets were always out-based at Swansea. Class 120 cross-country sets, and later Class 101 Met-Cam sets, were used on the Central Wales line and in West Wales. On 5 November 1980, two Class 120 sets are stabled at Maliphant DMU fuelling point in Swansea.

A view of the carriage sidings from the platform end at Swansea on 6 June 1983. Maliphant fuelling point is in the distance beyond the water tower. The carriage sidings pilot is Landore-allocated No. 08897. Also visible is Class 101 Met-Cam power-twin set C804, formed of vehicle Nos 51452 and 51523.

At Swansea on 28 July 1980, Class 120 set C605 (formed of vehicle Nos 50733 and 50686) is departing on the 14.58 Central Wales line service to Shrewsbury. At the time, there were six Class 120 power-twin sets fitted with headlights for the Central Wales route. By 1982 they had been replaced by Class 101 power-twin sets.

A busy scene at Swansea on 7 July 1981, with three platforms occupied. Canton-allocated No. 47105 stands in platform 4. On platform 3 Canton-allocated No. 37186 waits to work the 11.15 service to Milford Haven. The HST set will work the 11.42 departure for Paddington.

In 1980, thirteen of the Landore allocation of Class 37s were fitted with steam heating boilers, and these were also used on passenger services in West Wales. On 28 July 1980, one of the allocation, No. 37179, awaits departure time at Swansea with a service for Fishguard Harbour.

Once Class 33s had taken over loco-hauled workings in West Wales in 1982, no steam heating loco diagrams remained – most of the Landore boiler-fitted Class 37s had been allocated elsewhere. On 6 June 1983, Old Oak Common-allocated Class 47 No. 47536 is seen at the head of the 10.17 Swansea to Fishguard Harbour.

By 1986, as well as working passenger services in West Wales, the Class 33s also worked two services each weekday to Portsmouth Harbour. On 19 September 1986, Hither Green-allocated Slim Jim Class 33/2 No. 33205 stands at Swansea, waiting to work the 09.50 service to Portsmouth Harbour.

The remaining two Class 120 DMU sets had left South Wales by 1986. The Canton DMU allocation now included twelve Class 101 Met-Cam sets, nine of them power-twin sets. On 19 September, three-car set C814 stands at Swansea, formed of vehicle Nos 53319, 59123, and 53335.

Swansea Burrows Sidings was a busy yard. As well as handling export coal through Swansea Docks there were a number of freight terminals and private sidings close by. On 5 November 1980, No. 47249 stands beside Burrows Sidings signal box.

A large number of unfitted 21-ton minerals had been re-bodied in the 1970s. They became MDOs on the TOPS system, and many of them were employed to convey export coal traffic through Swansea Docks. On 19 September 1986, a train of export coal from Onllwyn, loaded in MDOs, has just arrived at Swansea Burrows behind No. 37506.

The rail network in the Swansea Docks area had been very complex. Despite the weeds and decay, a number of freight customers remained at Gower Chemicals, Port Tennant Wagon Repairs, and the Eastern Coal Depot. On 9 November 1983, Burrows yard pilot No. 08769 runs past the decaying Ashland Chemicals plant.

A small fleet of seventeen tank cars had been modified for use conveying sulphuric acid from ISC Chemicals at Hallen Marsh to various terminals; Gower Chemicals at Swansea was one of the customers. The tanks sometimes also visited the Marcroft wagon repair depot at Port Tennant for maintenance. On 19 September 1986, pilot No. 08780 brings a single sulphuric acid TTA from the Marcroft wagon works into Swansea Burrows.

On 19 September 1986, shortly after arriving at Swansea Burrows with a train of export coal, No. 37506 has been detached from the train and has drawn up beside Swansea Burrows signal box. The loco had recently been refurbished and modified to Class 37/5 and is carrying the new Railfreight grey livery. It was formerly No. 37007.

The MDOs of export coal, which had recently arrived from Onllwyn on 19 September 1986, are now being hauled into Swansea Docks by Swansea Burrows pilot No. 08780. The wagons will go into the holding sidings to await their turn for unloading.

The view from Fabian Way road overbridge, looking west into the Swansea Docks on 9 November 1983. One of the two Class 08 pilots on duty in the docks that day, No. 08259 is hauling two empty MDOs out of the holding sidings. The use of MDOs on this traffic continued until 1987 and was the last revenue-earning traffic to use this type of wagon.

On 9 November 1983, Swansea Docks pilot No. 08259 hauls a short rake of seven loaded MDOs out of the holding sidings. Wagons loaded with export coal had to be uncoupled and shunted singly onto the hoists for unloading so unfitted wagons were preferred for this traffic. The complex track layout is controlled by Kings Dock Junction signal box.

Dockside cranes and coal hoists form the backdrop as dock pilot No. 08367 propels MDOs of export coal towards the hoists on 19 September 1986. The use of MDOs on export coal through Swansea Docks continued until early 1987. After that, coal to Ireland was mostly containerised.

Swansea Docks pilot No. 08259 draws MDOs of export coal out of the East End sidings on 9 November 1983. Note how the wagons are arranged with the end door facing west; this facilitates the unloading procedure on the coal hoists.

On 15 June 1983, No. 47478 races past Llandeilo Junction yard with the 17.55 Swansea to Carmarthen service. The postal vans in the formation will be attached to the nightly postal service to Bristol Temple Meads. The background is dominated by the British Steel tinplate works at Trostre, an important BR freight customer.

A lengthy train of 21-ton mineral wagons heads west through Llanelli on 24 June 1982. The loco is No. 37266, its centre lamp bracket being a legacy of the time the loco was allocated to Stratford, although by the date of this photo the loco was allocated to Landore.

The prototype Class 140 set No. 140001, which is formed of vehicle Nos 55500 and 55501, stands at Llanelli on 24 June 1982. It is working the 15.00 service from Swansea to Shrewsbury, via the Central Wales route. This set carried out trials on many routes across the network.

By the summer of 1982 Class 101 Met-Cam sets had taken over much of the local work in West Wales. On 24 June 1982, two Class 101 sets call at Llanelli, working the 16.10 service from Swansea to Pembroke Dock via Carmarthen, where one of the sets will be detached. Set C800 is formed of vehicle Nos 51445 and 51515; set C803 is formed of vehicle Nos 51450 and 51522.

Carmarthen Bay power station forms the backdrop as the 13.00 service from Swansea to Milford Haven departs Pembrey and Burry Port on 15 June 1983. By this date only two Swindon-built cross-country DMU sets remained allocated to Cardiff Canton. Set C615 is formed of vehicle Nos 51781, 59682, and 51788. The power station received coal by rail but ceased generating in 1984.

The Landore-allocated Class 03 shunters are most often associated with Pembrey and Burry Port. However, on 15 June 1983 No. 08354, one of the Landore-allocated Class 08s, is seen shunting MDOs of coal in the yard at Burry Port.

To work the Burry Port and Gwendraeth Valley line to Cwmmawr colliery, which had limited clearance at a number of points, Landore depot had an allocation of modified Class 03 shunters. The modifications included cut-down cabs, headlights, and multiple working equipment. At Burry Port yard on 15 June 1983, locos Nos 03141, 03145, and 03152 have recently arrived with a train of MDOs of coal.

A general view of Burry Port yard looking east on 15 June 1983; the branch to Cwmmawr leads off to the right. Approaching Pembrey and Burry Port station is the 10.53 Swansea to Milford Haven service. Set C813 is one of nine three-car Class 101 Met-Cam sets allocated to Cardiff at the time. It is formed of vehicle Nos 53304, 59122, and 53329

Class 101 set C813 stands in Pembrey and Burry Port while working the 10.53 Swansea to Milford Haven service on 15 June 1983. No. 33029 passes through light diesel. The Class 33s had been working services in West Wales since May 1982.

The passenger train service to and from Fishguard Harbour was sparse, comprising three or four loco-hauled trains each way. On 15 June 1983, Bescot-allocated No. 47434 calls at Pembrey and Burry Port with the 14.45 service from Fishguard Harbour to Swansea.

One of the two remaining Cardiff-allocated Class 120 DMU sets is seen running into Carmarthen on 6 June 1983. Set C616 (formed of vehicle Nos 51782, 59681, and 51790) is working the 10.53 Swansea to Milford Haven service. On the left, in Carmarthen yard, the presflos are standing in the Aberthaw Cement terminal.

A view across Carmarthen station on 6 June 1983 as a Class 101 Met-Cam DMU set calls, forming the 10.02 service from Pembroke Dock to Swansea. Power-twin set C804 is formed of vehicle Nos 51452 and 51523. No. 47536 had recently arrived at Carmarthen with the 10.17 service from Swansea to Fishguard Harbour.

Looking north across the River Towy at Carmarthen on 6 June 1983, and an unidentified Class 37 loco stands in the goods yard. The goods yard was located at the former Carmarthen Town station, which had closed to passenger services in the 1960s and would also close to goods traffic in 1983.

Whitland is the junction for the branch to Pembroke Dock, which is single-track with a crossing loop at Tenby. On 6 June 1983, the Whitland signalman is about to hand over the token for the single-line section to Tenby. Class 120 cross-country set C616 is working the 17.31 service to Pembroke Dock.

The 16.10 Pembroke Dock to Swansea service calls at Whitland, formed by Class 101 Met-Cam set C802, on 6 June 1983. Power-twin set C802 is formed of vehicle Nos 51449 and 51521. On weekdays there were seven trains a day to Pembroke Dock, with another that terminated at Tenby.

On 6 June 1983, Class 101 Met-Cam set C804 calls at Haverfordwest with the 13.00 service from Swansea to Milford Haven. In 1983 there were eleven passenger services each way on weekdays on the Milford Haven route. These were worked by a mixture of DMUs and loco-hauled stock.

One of the Canton-allocated named Class 47s, No. 47089 *Amazon*, heads through Haverfordwest on 6 June 1983. It is returning light diesel from one of the Milford Haven oil refineries. In 1983 there was also a daily Speedlink trip working from Llandeilo Junction to Milford Haven that called at Haverfordwest.

Class 101 Met-Cam set C804 is seen at Haverfordwest, returning on the 15.25 service from Milford Haven to Swansea. Set C804 was one of seven power-twin Class 101 sets allocated to Cardiff at the time, though they spent most of their time in West Wales, working on services out of Swansea.

Pantyffynnon on the Central Wales line was a hub for coal traffic from several collieries in the area, and a number of locos were out-based there. On 4 November 1983, No. 08799 is seen adjacent to Pantyffynnon signal box, returning to the yard having just moved MDOs of coal from Betws Drift mine to Wernos Washery.

A number of the Class 101 Met-Cam sets had previously been based at Bristol. On 24 June 1982, set B802 is still showing that it had been a Bristol-allocated set, being formed of vehicle Nos 51449 and 51521. The set is seen calling at Pantyffynnon on the 10.08 Swansea to Shrewsbury service, via the Central Wales route.

Class 101 set C801 (formed of vehicle Nos 51446 and 51517) approaches Pantyffynnon on the 10.50 Shrewsbury to Swansea service on 4 November 1983. The train is passing the exchange sidings for Wernos Washery, which are full of MDOs loaded with coal.

Three Landore-allocated locos are seen in the loco stabling point adjacent to Pantyffynnon station on 24 June 1982. Pilot No. 08660 is attached to a rake of MDOs, while Nos 37267 and 37304 stand in the yard. The shoc-van in the yard was in use as a store for bags of loco sand. The loco sand was used by the Class 37 drivers to help control the heavy unfitted coal trains on the steeply graded routes in the area.

In the 1980s there was sufficient work in the Pantyffynnon area to require two Landore-allocated Class 08 pilot locos to be out-based there. In this view looking south on 4 November 1983, No. 08799 is nearer the camera, while No. 08662 is coupled to the brake van beside the station.

Also available from Amberley Publishing

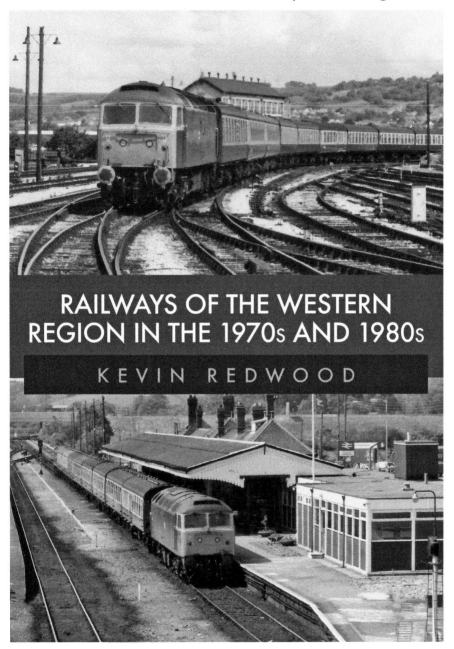

RAILWAYS OF THE WESTERN REGION IN THE 1970s AND 1980s

KEVIN REDWOOD

Also available from Amberley Publishing

RAILWAYS OF THE WEST OF ENGLAND IN THE 1980s

KEVIN REDWOOD

Available from all good bookshops or to order direct
Please call **01453-847-800**
www.amberley-books.com